BEADED NECKLACE ANI

by Marie Le Fevre

YOU WILL NEED:

dark blue suede lacing: 4 yards (necklace), 2/3 yard (earrings)
silver pony beads: 142 (necklace), 8 (earrings)
1" wide round nickel concho
1 pair of silver French clip earring posts
ruler
scissors

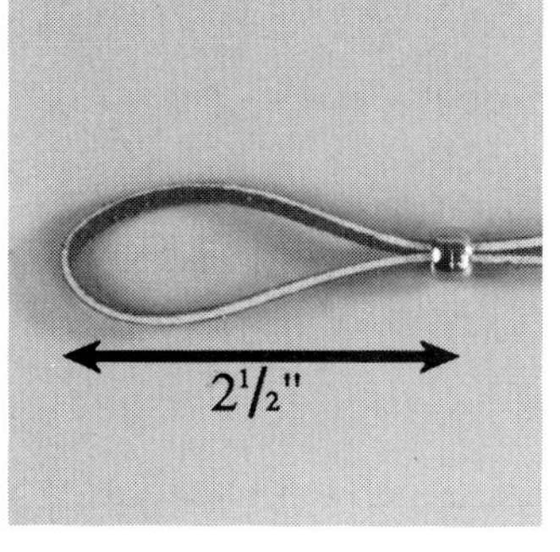

1

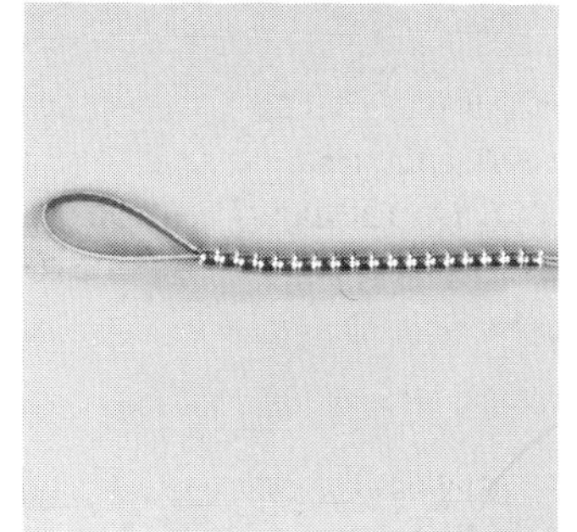

2

1 **For the necklace:** Cut a 48" lacing length and fold it in half. Insert the ends through a bead and slide the bead up to 2½" from the folded end.

2 Thread on 17 more beads. Slide each up next to the last.

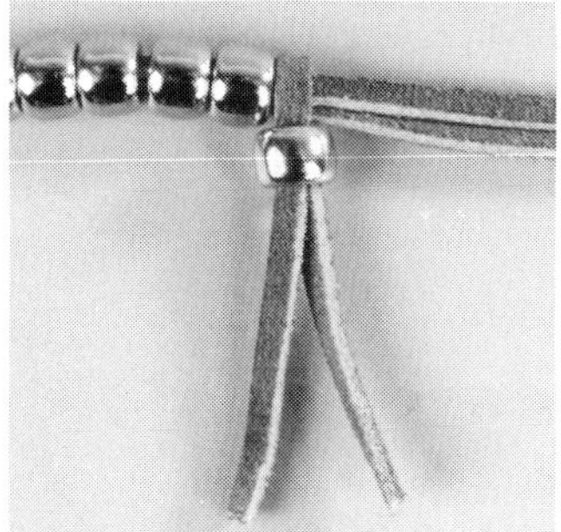

3

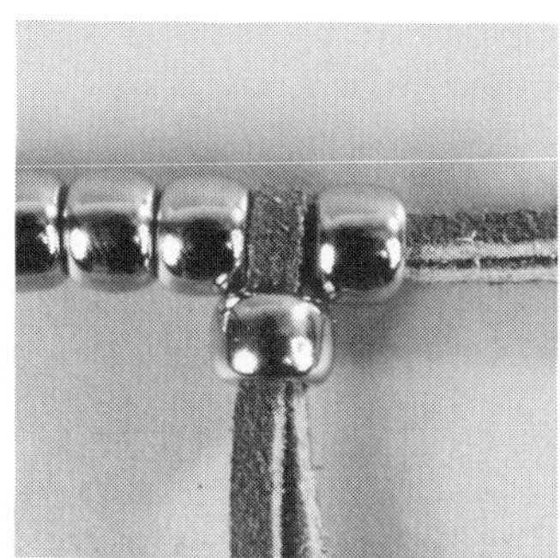

4

3 Cut the remaining lacing into the following lengths: two 12", two 10", two 8", two 6", and six 4". Fold a 4" length in half around the center of the 48" length. Insert the ends through a bead and slide it up to secure the lacing. Slide the lacing up next to the previous beads.

4 Thread another bead onto the 48" length, sliding it up next to the 4" length.

5

6 back view

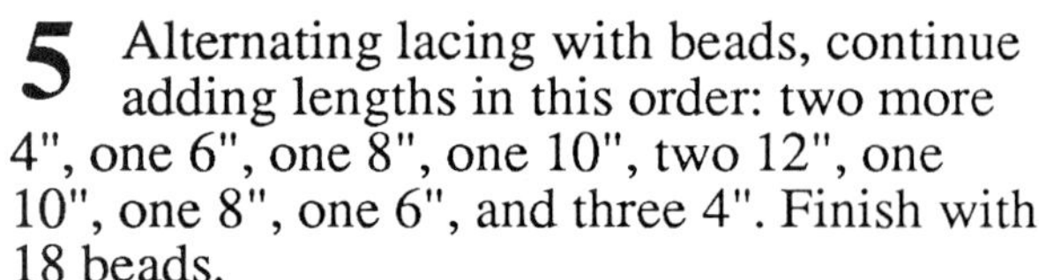

5 Alternating lacing with beads, continue adding lengths in this order: two more 4", one 6", one 8", one 10", two 12", one 10", one 8", one 6", and three 4". Finish with 18 beads.

6 Thread both cut ends of the 48" lacing from back to front through the concho, then back through. Slide the concho up to the beads. Knot the lacing lengths together $2\frac{1}{2}$" from the last bead, then slide the concho back to the knot.

7

8

7 Slide a bead onto each end of the 48" length, then knot the ends of the lacing to secure the beads.

8 Follow the diagram to string the remaining beads onto the lacing. Leave $\frac{1}{4}$" between each row of beads.

9

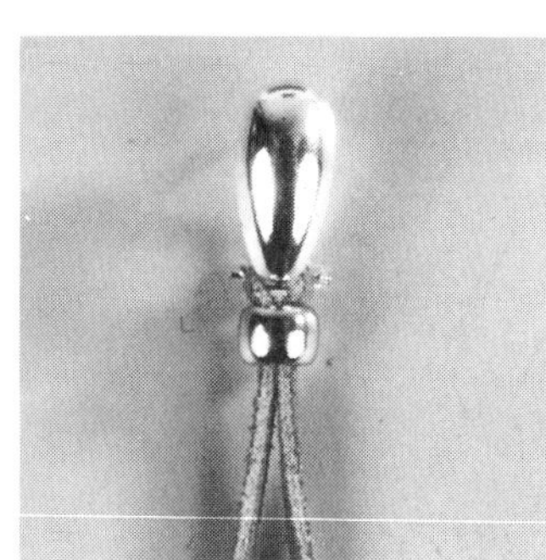

10

9 To clasp the necklace: Slip the loop end over the concho, leaving the beaded ends hanging free.

10 **For each earring:** Cut two 6" lacing lengths. Insert one around the hinge of an ear post so the ends extend equally. Insert the ends through a bead and slide it up as high as it will go.

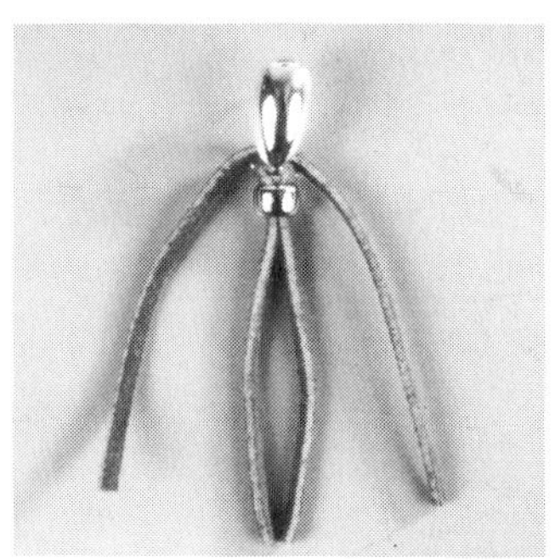

11

12

11 Insert the second lacing length over the first, adjusting the ends to extend equally.

12 Follow the diagram to string the remaining beads.

LACY CONCHO PIN & BRAID BRACELET

by E. Wayne Fox

YOU WILL NEED:

for the lacy concho pin:
24" length of pink suede lacing
2 1/4"x2 7/8" oval antique nickel concho
pony beads: 8 light turquoise, 8 silver
6 pink heart pony beads
1/4 yard of 3/4" wide cream gathered lace
1" long pin back
E-6000™ glue

for the braid bracelet:
1 yard of pink suede lacing
four 5/8"x3/4" oval nickel concho press-on studs
1 silver pony bead
masking tape

1 **For the lacy concho pin:** Glue the pin to the concho bar. Cut a 1" length of lace and glue it to the back, covering the upper opening. Glue the bound edge of the remaining lace around the back edge of the concho.

2 Cut the lacing into two 12" lengths. Hold them together, fold them in half, and insert the fold back to front through the lower concho slot. Insert all the tails back to front through the upper slot, then bring them down through the loop (lark's head knot). Pull the lower edge of the lace to the front and glue it to the lacing. Thread beads on one outside tail in this order: turquoise, silver, heart, silver, and turquoise. Knot the lacing end. Repeat for the remaining tails, but use two heart beads on the two inner tails as shown in the large photo.

3 **For the braid bracelet:** Shape the lacing into a large loop, with the ends extending 3". Tape the overlapped end to the table (see diagram). Braid the long end and loop strands together tightly. Be sure to keep the lacing flat—the loop will twist and untwist as you braid. When the loop becomes small, finish by passing the end through it and pulling it tight. Untape the other end and pull it tight also.

4 Space the studs evenly along the braid and secure by pressing the prongs through. Bend the prongs down on the back, pressing them tightly into the braid. Finish by passing the ends through the bead from opposite sides. Knot each end. Adjust the bracelet by pulling the ends in opposite directions.

1 back view

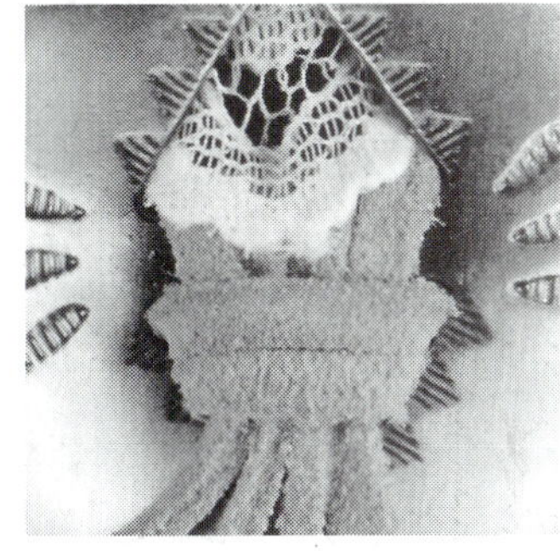

2

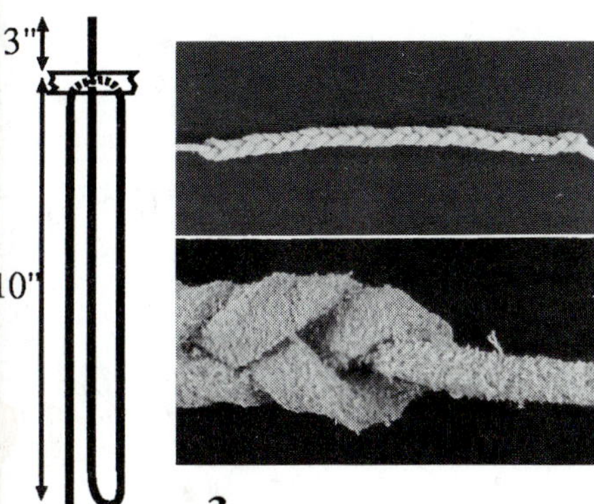

3

4 back view

BRAIDED NECKLACE AND EARRINGS

by Marie Le Fevre

YOU WILL NEED:

suede lacing: 2 1/4 yards of peach, 3 yards of turquoise, 2 1/4 yards of beige (necklace); 1/2 yard of beige (earrings)
pony beads: 16 silver, 13 cream (necklace); 2 silver, 4 cream (earrings)
Moroccan pony beads: 3 silver, 3 terra cotta, 3 turquoise (necklace); 2 turquoise (earrings)

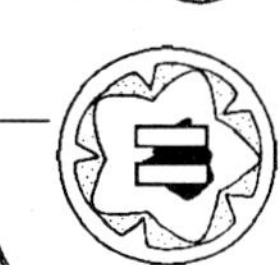

melon pony beads: 6 silver, 3 terra cotta, 3 turquoise (necklace); 2 terra cotta (earrings)
four 1" wide round nickel conchos (necklace)
2 silver fishhook ear wires
ruler
scissors
masking tape
leather glue

1

2

1 Cut a 36" length each of peach, beige and turquoise lacing. Tape one end of each to the table and braid for 11"; tape just above the bottom of the braid to secure it.

2 Separate the lacing ends. Cut the following lacing lengths: 13" each of beige and turquoise; 14" each of beige and peach; 15" each of turquoise and peach. Glue one end of each 13" length to the braided peach strand at the bottom of the braid. Glue one end of each 14" length to the turquoise strand, and one end of each 15" length to the beige strand.

3

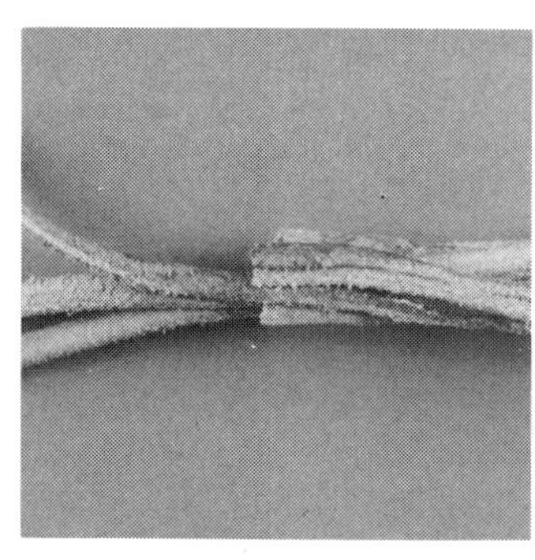

4

glue

3 Separate the three strand groups—each should have one long strand (from the braid) and two shorter strands. Set aside seven silver and two cream pony beads for steps 6, 9 and 10. Thread the remaining beads at random onto the strands, knotting them as needed to keep beads in place. Large beads may be strung onto two strands, but be careful to keep the three groups separate.

4 Gather all the strands and glue them together where the short ends meet (see diagram). The braid tails will extend.

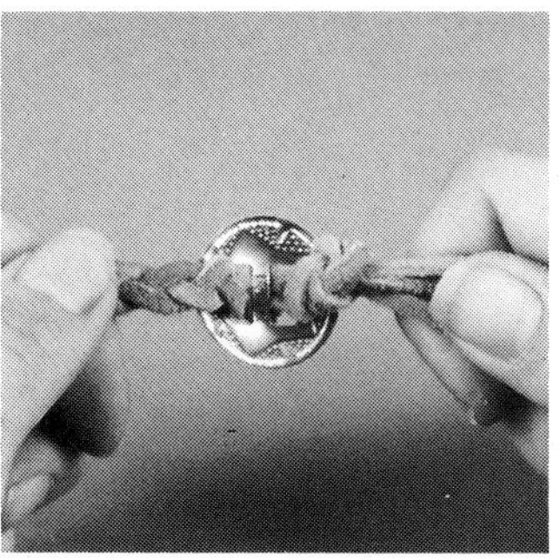
5 back view

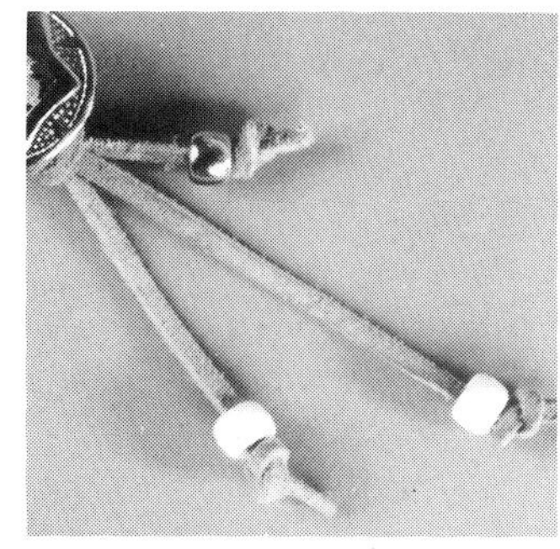
6

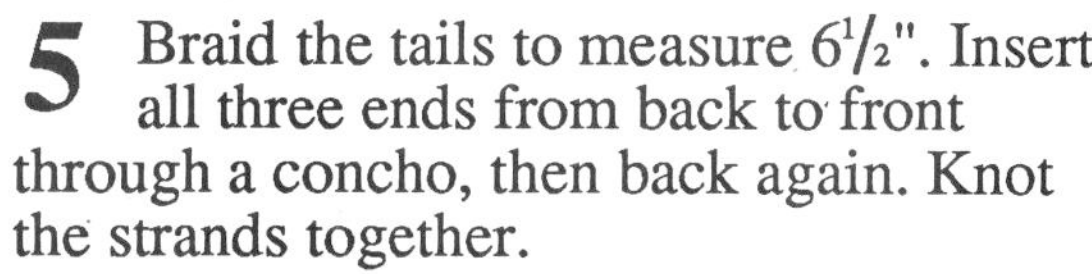
5 Braid the tails to measure $6\frac{1}{2}$". Insert all three ends from back to front through a concho, then back again. Knot the strands together.

6 Insert the turquoise end through a silver bead and knot to secure. Insert each remaining end through a cream bead and knot to secure.

7

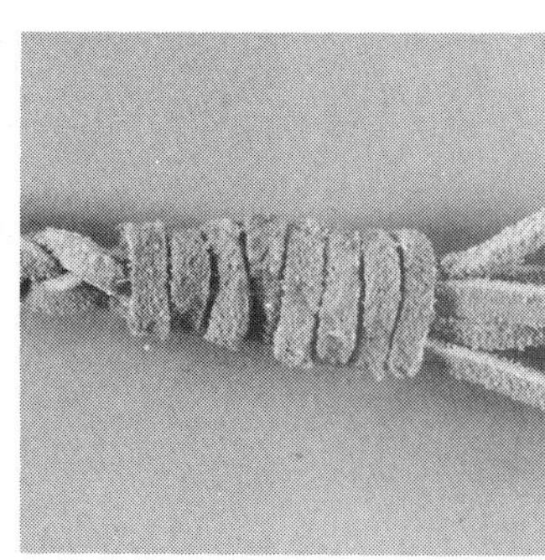
8

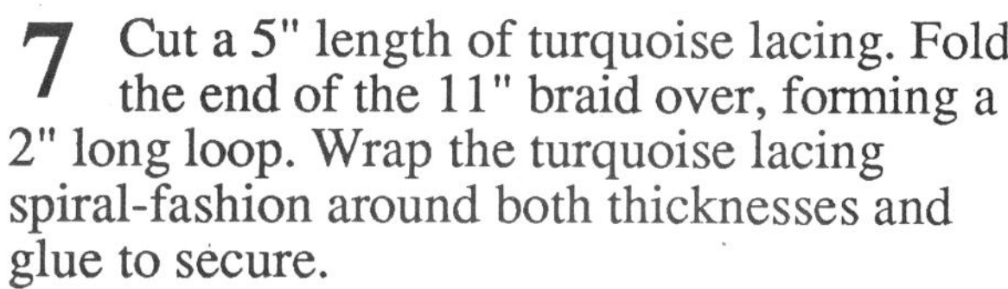
7 Cut a 5" length of turquoise lacing. Fold the end of the 11" braid over, forming a 2" long loop. Wrap the turquoise lacing spiral-fashion around both thicknesses and glue to secure.

8 Cut two 10" lengths of turquoise lacing. Wrap and glue one to cover the glued area between the braid and the short strands. Glue the other to cover the glued area on the opposite side.

9

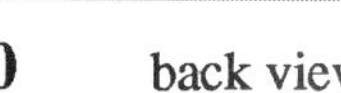

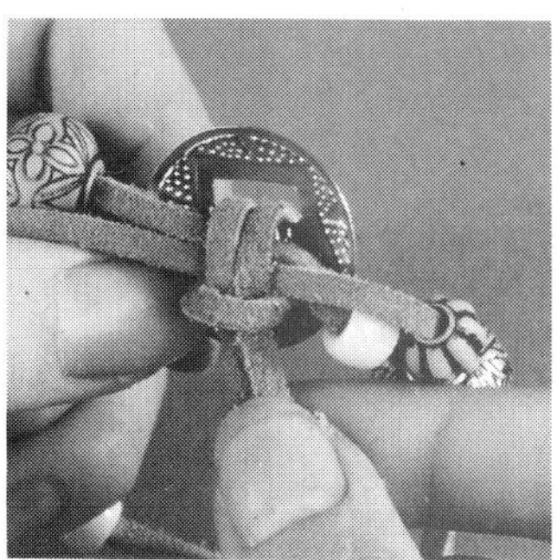
10 back view

9 Cut a 10" length of turquoise lacing. Insert each end through a silver bead, then knot. Fold in half and insert the fold from back to front through a concho, then through the other slot to the back. Place the concho over the center of the lowest 3-strand group (see diagram).

10 On the back, insert the beaded ends through the fold (lark's head knot). Pull the ends to tighten the lacing around the strands. Repeat with a beige length near the right end of the center strand group, then with a peach length near the left end of the upper strand group.

11

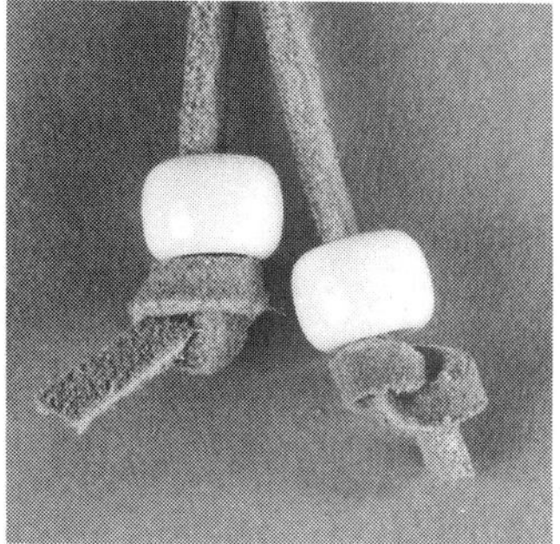
12

11 **For each earring:** Cut an 8" length of beige lacing. Insert through the eye of an ear wire so the ends extend equally. Insert the ends through a turquoise Moroccan bead, then through a silver pony bead and a terra cotta melon bead. Slide all the beads as high as they will go.

12 Insert a cream bead onto each lacing end, knotting the lacing to secure the beads.

DESK SET

by Marie Le Fevre

YOU WILL NEED:

ruler, scissors, leather glue, E-6000™ glue

for the box:

$3\frac{7}{8}$"x$1\frac{3}{4}$" chipwood box with lid

suede lacing: $3\frac{1}{2}$ yards each of violet, dark blue, pink; 3 yards of mauve

$1\frac{5}{8}$"x$2\frac{1}{4}$" antique nickel concho —

3 cream pony beads

4" square of violet felt

for the pencil holder:

$3\frac{1}{4}$"x$3\frac{1}{4}$" can

suede lacing: 2 yards each of violet, dark blue, mauve, and pink; $1\frac{1}{3}$ yards of peach

$1\frac{5}{8}$"x$2\frac{1}{4}$" antique nickel concho (see above)

3 silver pony beads

4" square of violet felt

for the paperweight:

smooth oval rock, about 1"x$3\frac{1}{2}$"x4"

suede lacing: exact yardage will depend on the rock size; used here, $1\frac{1}{2}$ yards of beige, $1\frac{3}{4}$ yards of burgundy, $2\frac{1}{2}$ yards of mauve

$2\frac{1}{4}$" wide round nickel concho —

4 silver pony beads

1 back view

2 back view

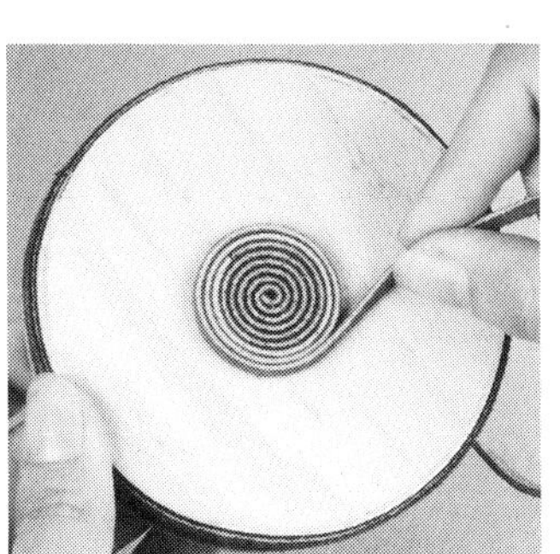

3

4

1 **For the box:** Set the lid aside for step 2. Glue the felt to the bottom and trim it to fit. Beginning at the bottom, wrap and glue 24" of violet lacing around the box, with each wrap touching the previous one. Repeat with blue, mauve, and pink.

2 Glue a band of mauve lacing around the lower side of the lid; cut off excess. Repeat for a band of blue and two of violet.

3 Mark the center point of the lid top. Cut a 9" violet length and coil it, gluing to secure each coil. Glue to the lid center. Cut an 18" mauve length. Coil it around the violet, gluing the edges to the lid top. Repeat with a 27" blue length, 36" pink length, 45" mauve length, and 54" blue length.

4 Cut three 6" pink lengths and a 3" violet length. Insert the pink lengths front to back through the top concho slot, then back through the bottom, adjusting the ends as shown. Wrap and glue the violet length around all the pink lengths close to the concho. Slide a cream bead onto one end of each pink length, knotting the lacing to secure the bead. Glue the concho to the center top of the lid.

5 back view

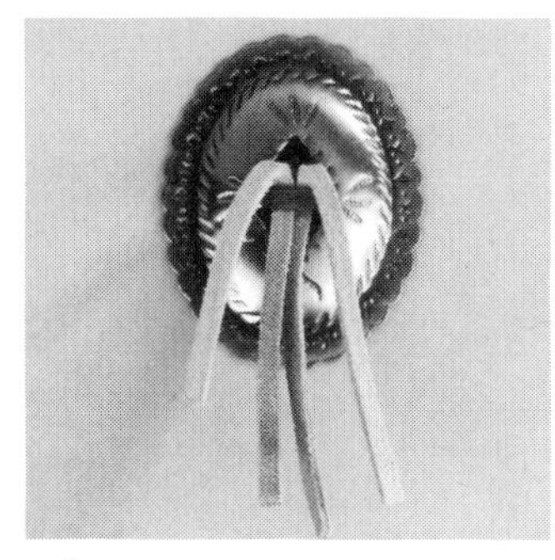
6

5 **For the pencil holder:** Beginning at the bottom, wrap and glue 36" of violet lacing around the can, with each wrap touching the previous one. Repeat wrapping and gluing in this order: blue, mauve, pink, peach, violet, blue mauve, and pink.

6 Cut two 5" lengths of peach lacing. Thread each around the bar of the concho, with the ends extending.

7

8

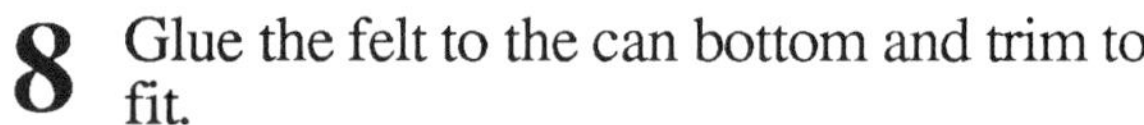
7 Follow the diagram to thread three silver beads onto the lacing ends. Glue the concho to the side of the can.

8 Glue the felt to the can bottom and trim to fit.

9

10 end view

9 **For the paperweight:** Wrap beige lacing diagonally around the center of the rock for three wraps. Glue to secure, then cut off excess lace. Glue burgundy for four wraps on the right side of the beige lacing, then repeat on the other side. Glue three more beige wraps on the right.

10 Wrap and glue mauve lacing to the end of the rock. The wraps will become successively smaller, until the last wraps are coiled inside one another. Repeat on the other end.

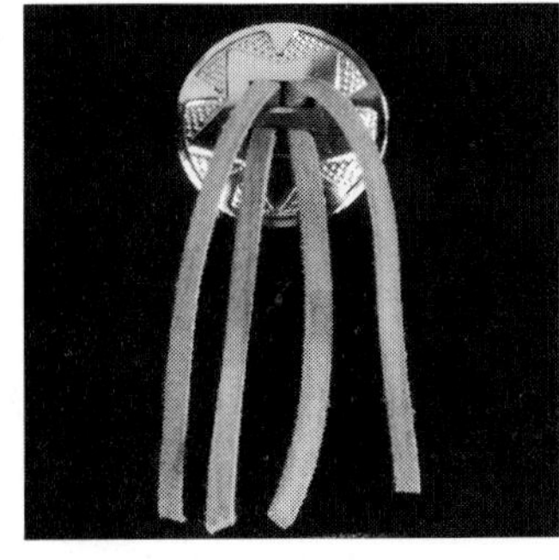

11

12

11 Cut two 6" lengths of beige lacing. Thread each around the bar of the concho, with the ends extending equally.

12 Follow the diagram to thread four silver beads onto the lacing ends. Glue the concho to the top of the paperweight.

FACE PIN

by Marie Le Fevre

YOU WILL NEED:

1½" tall porcelain-like resin face
3"x5" piece of smooth pink leather
2½"x4" piece of smooth turquoise leather
three 5mm clear rhinestones
two ¼" wide pink porcelain roses
1½" long pink feather
½" long pin back
tracing paper, pencil
warm water, bowl, paper towels
E-6000™ glue
scissors

front

hat: cut 1 pink

hatband: cut 1 turquoise

1

2

3

4

1 Trace the patterns and cut the leather pieces. Soak the hat piece in warm water until soft; towel off excess water. The leather should feel damp, not wet. Stretch the piece over the head, shaping it to the contour of the head. Pull the ends to the back, pleating them to reduce bulk, and glue in place.

2 Glue the hatband around the hat crown. Glue the feather over it, extending to the left. Roll the point of the hat upward, shaping a rounded brim, and glue to secure.

3 Gather the scarf into three pleats. Roll ½" of the gathered end up and glue to secure. Glue the scarf to the neck as shown. Drape the pleats gracefully and secure them with small amounts of glue.

4 Glue a porcelain rose into the roll of the scarf, with a rhinestone to the right of it, as shown in the large photo. Glue the remaining rhinestones and rose to the hat front as shown at left. Glue on the pin back.

scarf: cut 1 turquoise

FINGER CROCHET BRACELETS

by Marie Le Fevre

YOU WILL NEED:

for the purple bracelet *(A):*
1 yard of purple suede lacing
for the black and silver bracelet *(B):*
1 yard of round black leather lacing cord
4 silver melon pony beads
for the blue and copper bracelet *(C):*
1 yard of dark blue suede lacing
10 copper pony beads

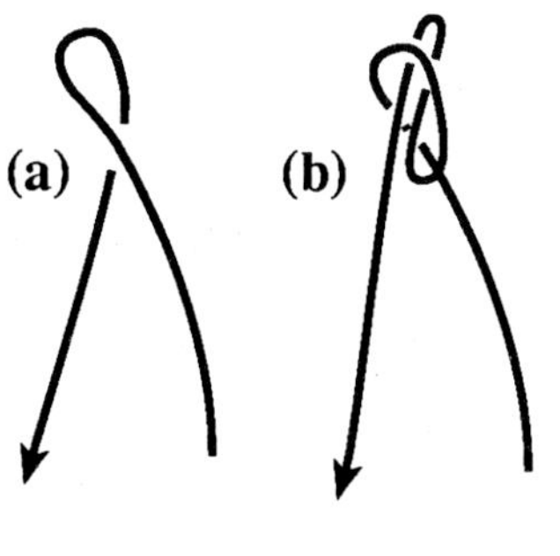

1

2

3

4

1 **For the purple bracelet (A):** (a) Form a 1" long loop in the lacing 4" from one end. The 4" tail should be on top. (b) Make a loop in the long end and push it through the first loop, front to back. Pull the first loop tight. Make another loop in the long end and push it through the second loop, pulling the second loop tight. Repeat until the crocheted portion measures 7" long—be careful to keep the lacing flat.

2 Pull the end of the lacing through the last loop and tighten the loop. Trim the tails to 2" and tie them together.

3 **For the black and silver bracelet (B):** Follow step 1 to crochet the black lacing for 3". Slide the beads onto the lacing, then form another loop as close as possible to them and continue crocheting for another 3". Trim the tails to 2" and tie them together.

4 **For the blue and copper bracelet (C):** Follow step 1 to crochet the blue lacing for 1½". Slip a bead onto the lacing, then crochet another loop. Slip on another bead and crochet another loop; continue until all ten beads have been crocheted in—if you keep the crocheting flat, the beads will fall on opposite sides. Crochet for another 1½" after the last bead. Trim the tails to 2" and tie them together.

LATTICE POINT NECKLACE

by E. Wayne Fox

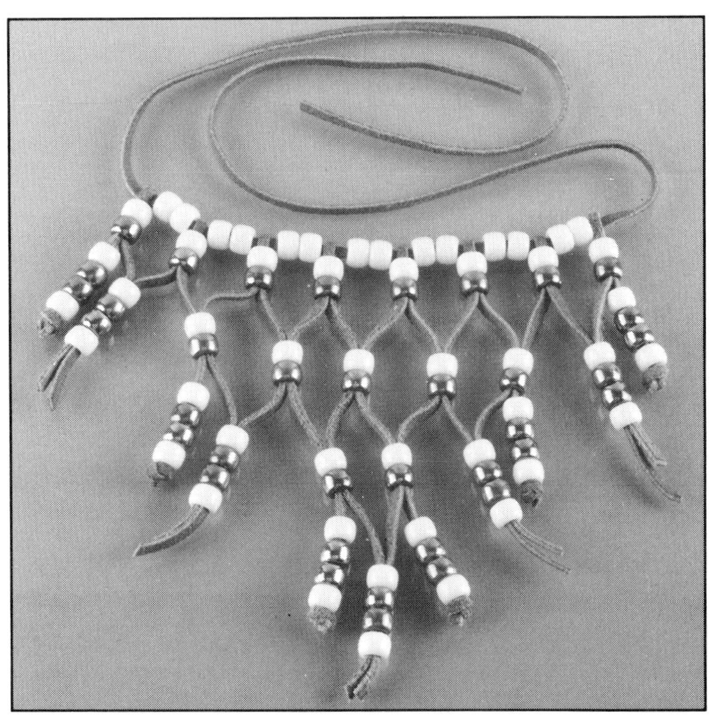

YOU WILL NEED:

3 yards of blue suede lacing
pony beads: 51 white, 37 gold
ruler
scissors

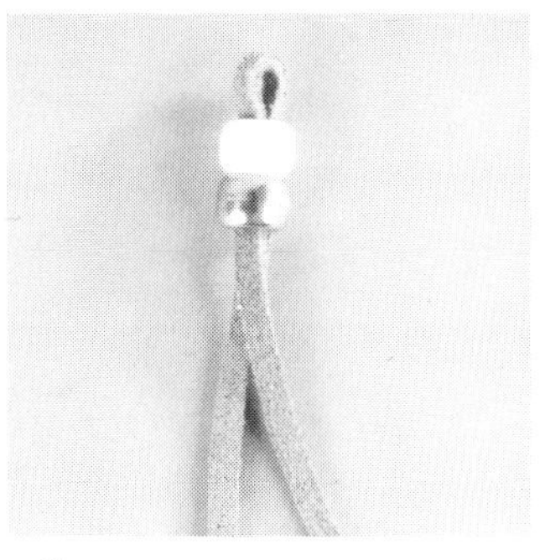

1

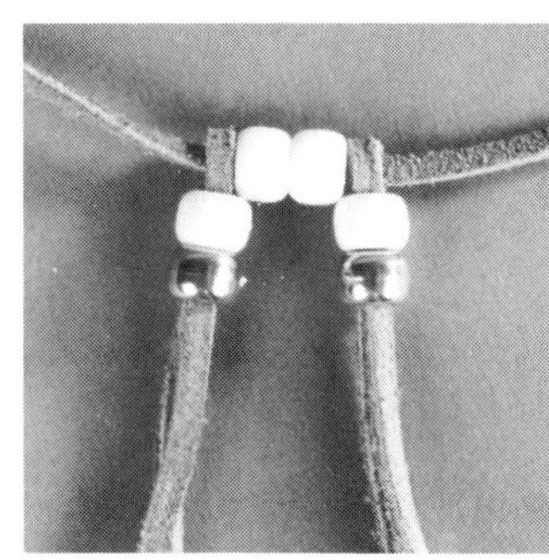

2

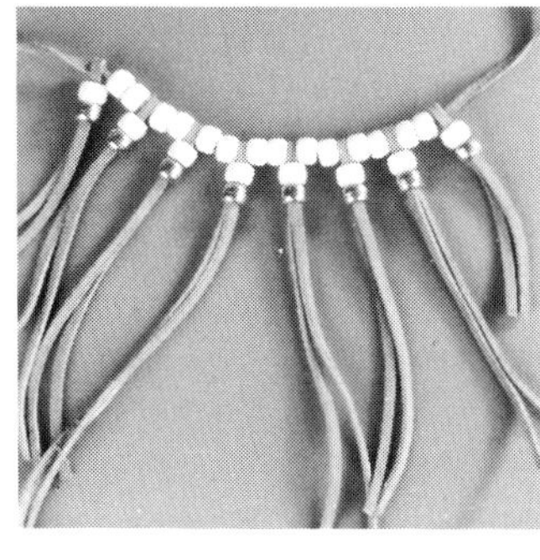

3

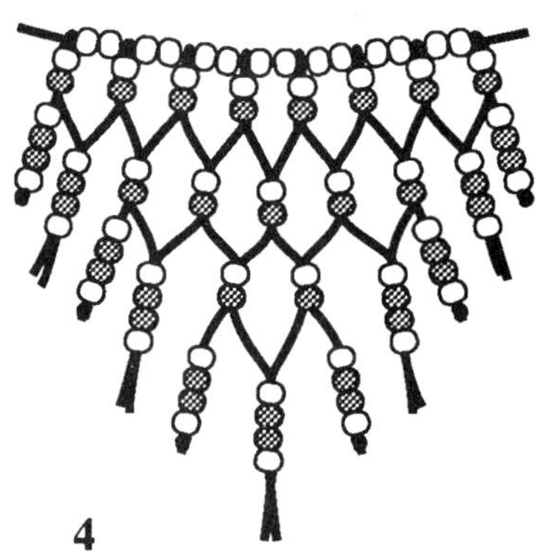

4

1 Cut the lacing to these lengths: one 27", two 13", four 10", and two 6". The 27" length will be the necklace, and the other lengths will be the fringe. Fold a fringe length in half. Slide a white bead over both ends and up until only a ¼" loop projects. Slide a gold bead over both ends and up to the white bead. Repeat for each fringe length.

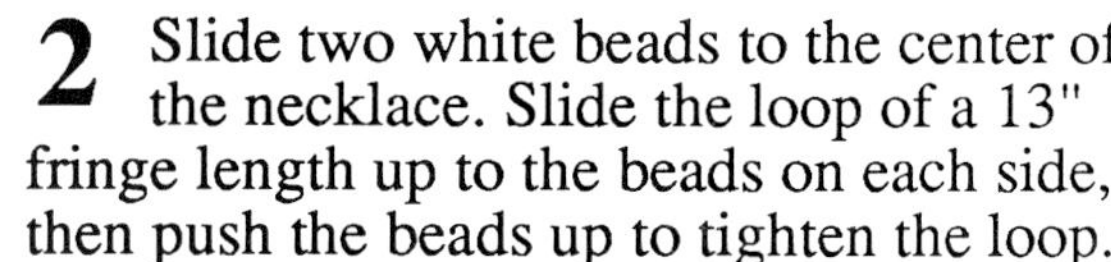

2 Slide two white beads to the center of the necklace. Slide the loop of a 13" fringe length up to the beads on each side, then push the beads up to tighten the loop.

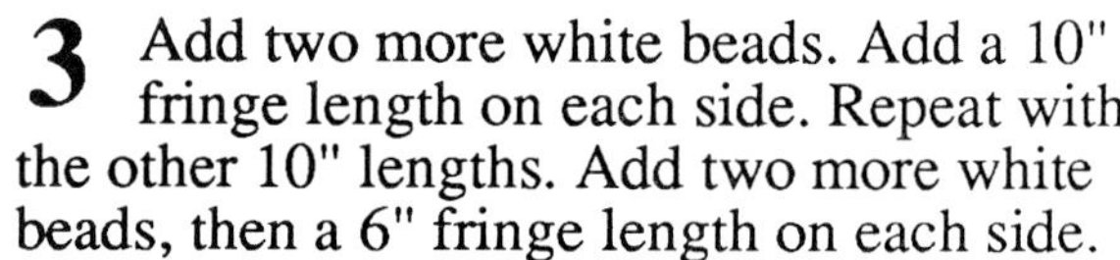

3 Add two more white beads. Add a 10" fringe length on each side. Repeat with the other 10" lengths. Add two more white beads, then a 6" fringe length on each side.

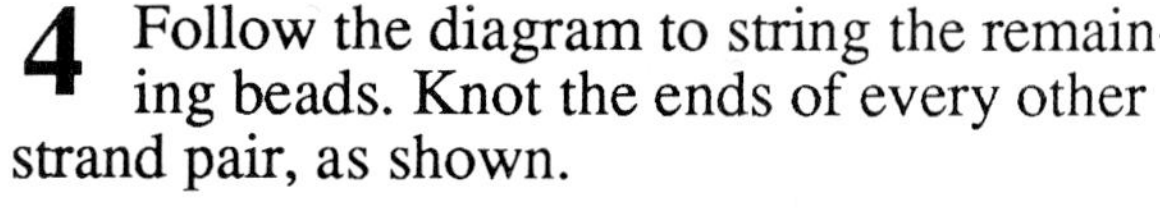

4 Follow the diagram to string the remaining beads. Knot the ends of every other strand pair, as shown.

BLUE COIL BELT

by Marie Le Fevre

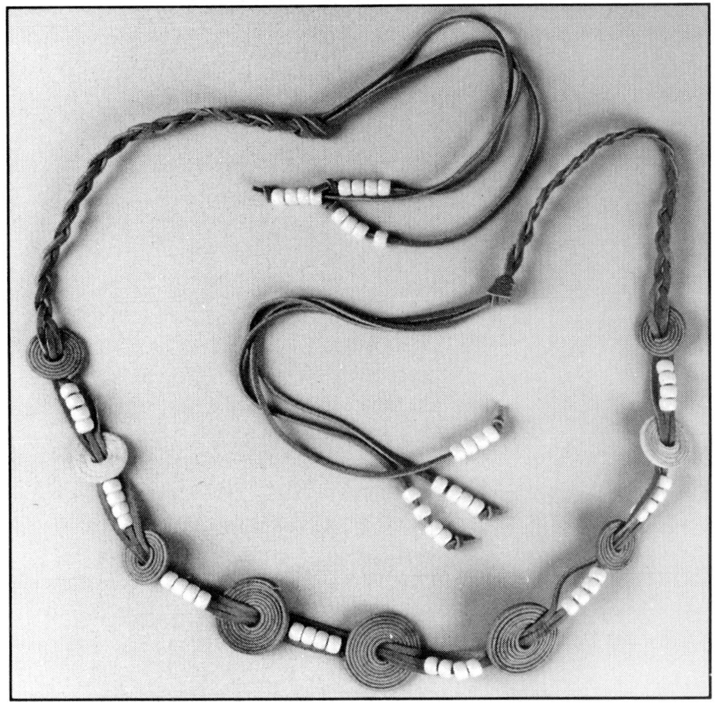

YOU WILL NEED:

suede lacing: 10 yards of blue, 20" of white
64 cream pony beads
3/8" wide dowel or pencil
ruler
scissors
leather glue

1

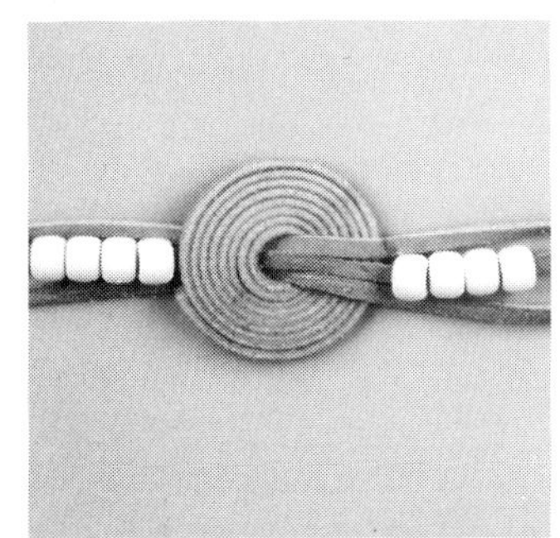

2

1 Cut the white lacing into two 10" lengths. Cut three 24" and four 10" lengths of blue. Coil each length around the dowel, gluing to secure each wrap. Remove, then let the glue dry.

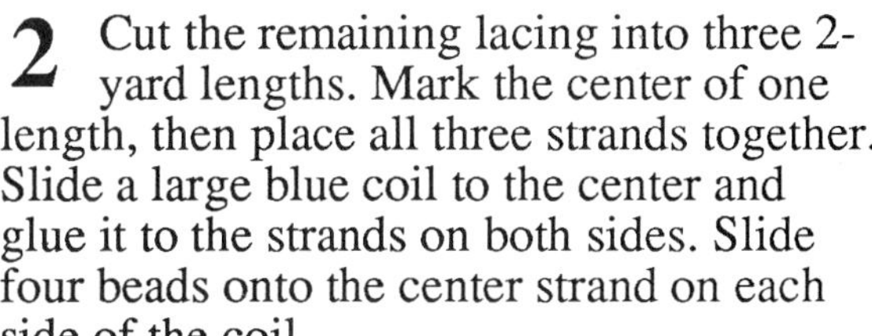

2 Cut the remaining lacing into three 2-yard lengths. Mark the center of one length, then place all three strands together. Slide a large blue coil to the center and glue it to the strands on both sides. Slide four beads onto the center strand on each side of the coil.

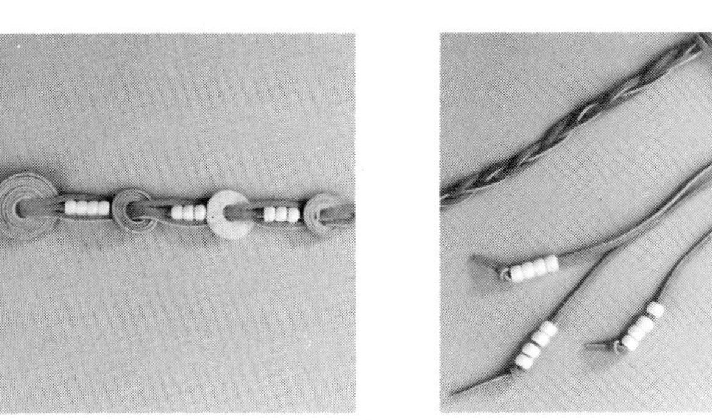

3

4

3 Slide another large blue coil over all three strands, positioning it so that the side that lies on top is toward the center. Glue in place, then add four more beads. In the same way, add a small blue coil, three beads, a white coil, three beads, and another small blue coil. Repeat on the other side.

4 To finish each end, braid the three strands together for 8" from the last coil. Knot the strands together below the braid. Slide four beads onto each strand; knot to secure.

MOSAIC BARRETTE AND BOLOS

by E. Wayne Fox

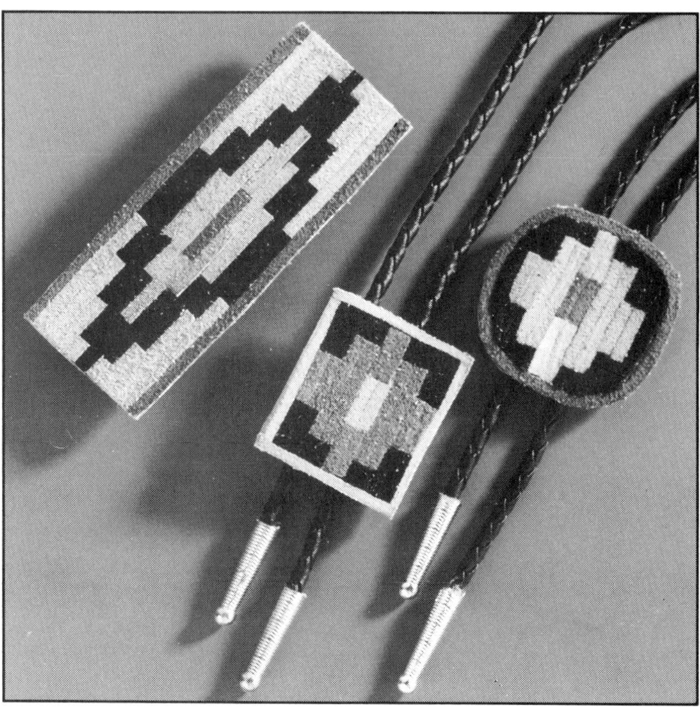

COLOR KEY: black mauve pink turquoise

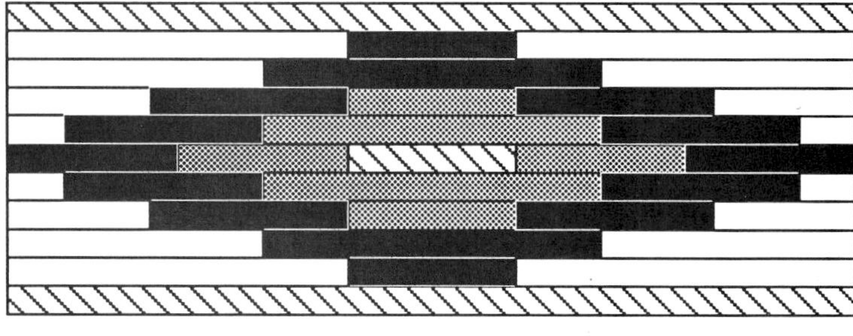

1

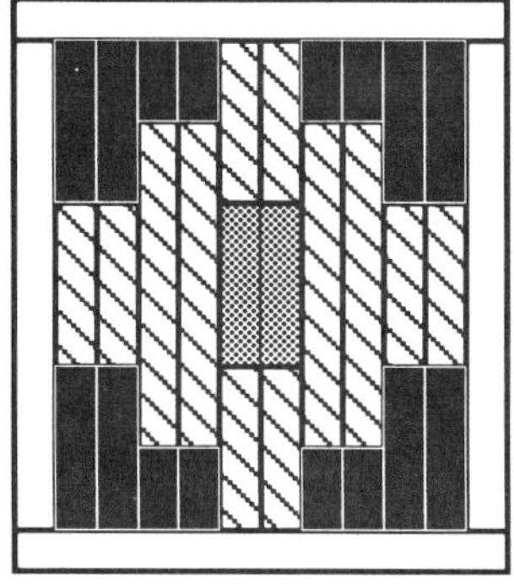

2

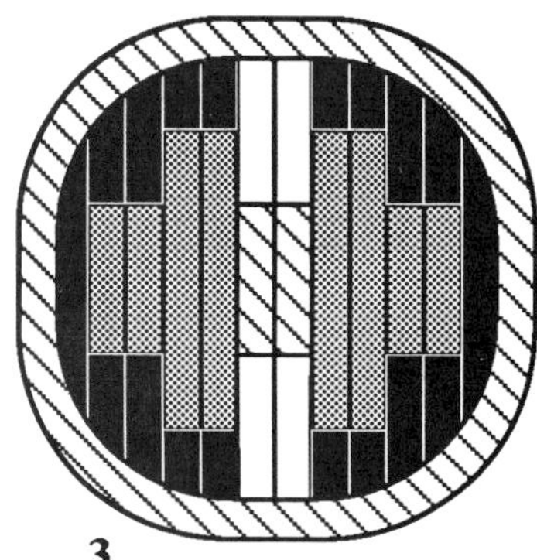

3

YOU WILL NEED:

leather glue, E-6000™ glue
pencil, ruler, X-acto® knife or scissors
for the barrette:
suede lacing: 13" of black, 8¼" of mauve, 12½" of pink, 6" of turquoise
1⅜"x3¾" piece of leather
2¾" long spring barrette clip
for the square bolo:
suede lacing: 6" of black, 6" of pink, 8" of mauve, 1" of turquoise
1½"x1¾" piece of stiff cardboard
36" long black braided leather bolo cord
2 brass bolo tips, bolo slide
for the round bolo:
suede lacing: 10¾" of black, 2" of pink, 7" of mauve, 3" of turquoise
1¾" rounded square of stiff cardboard (see pattern, step 3)
36" long black braided leather bolo cord
bolo slide, 2 nickel bolo tips

1 **Barrette:** Place the leather rectangle rough side up. Use the pencil and ruler to mark the horizontal and vertical centers. Cut the following lacing lengths:

black: two 1½", eight ⅞", four ¾"
mauve: two 3¾", one ¾"
pink: four 1½", four 1⅛", four ¾, four ¼"
turquoise: two 1½", four ¾"

Follow the diagram to glue the center row, then work upward and downward. Trim any uneven ends. Glue the barrette to the back.

2 **Square bolo:** Use the pencil and ruler to mark the centers of the cardboard. Cut the following lacing lengths:

black: eight ½", eight ¼"
mauve: four 1", eight ¼"
pink: four 1½"
turquoise: two ½"

Follow the diagram to glue the lacing to the cardboard; trim the ends. Glue the slide to the back. Insert the cord through the slide, then glue a tip on each cord end.

3 **Round bolo:** Make as for the square bolo, but use the following lacing lengths:

black: two 1", four ½", four ⅜", eight ¼"
mauve: one 6", two ½"
pink: four ½"
turquoise: two 1", two ½"

Trim the lacing ends in a smooth curve ⅛" inside the cardboard edge (an X-acto® knife works best). Glue the 6" mauve strip around the outer edge.

page 10

page 23

page 3

page 8

pages 9 and 19

page 24

page 22

page 11

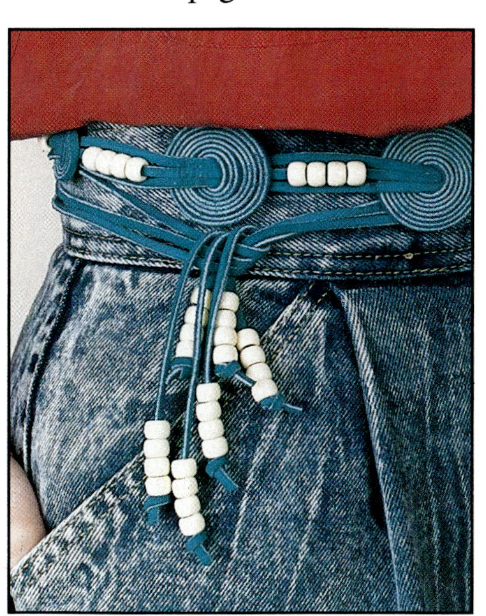

page 22

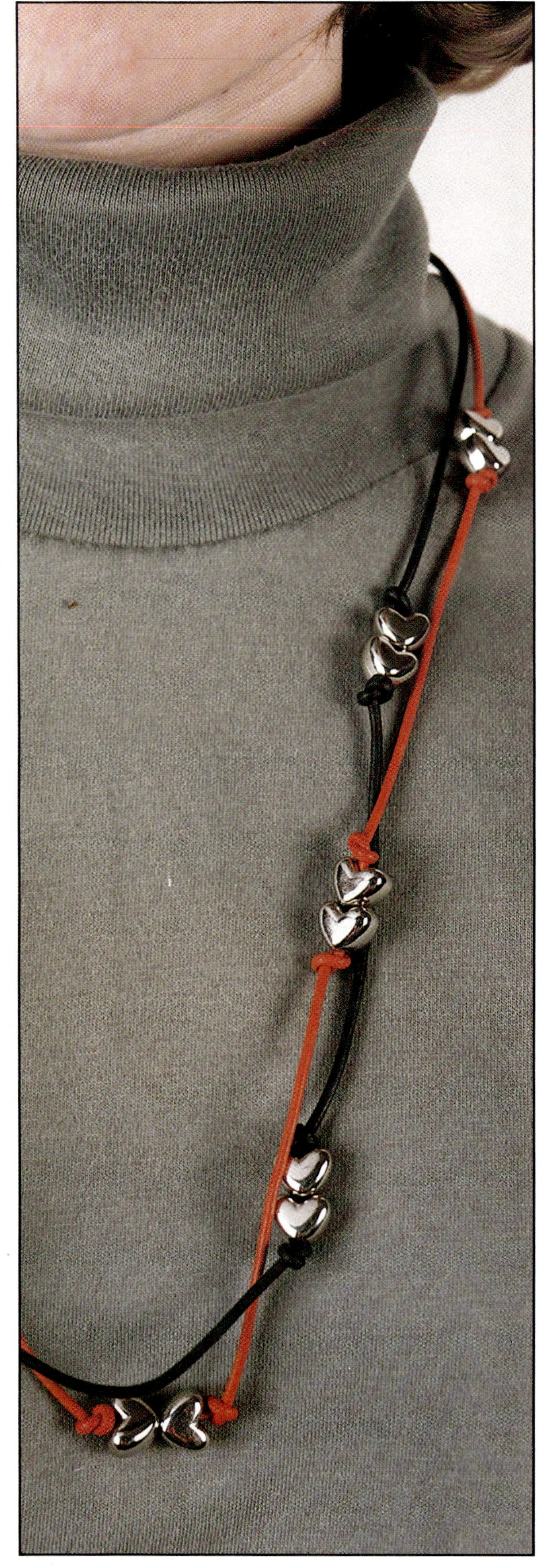

page 12

8

page 24

page 12

pages 26 and 27

pages 20 and 21

page 6

TWISTED NECKLACE AND EARRINGS

by Marie Le Fevre

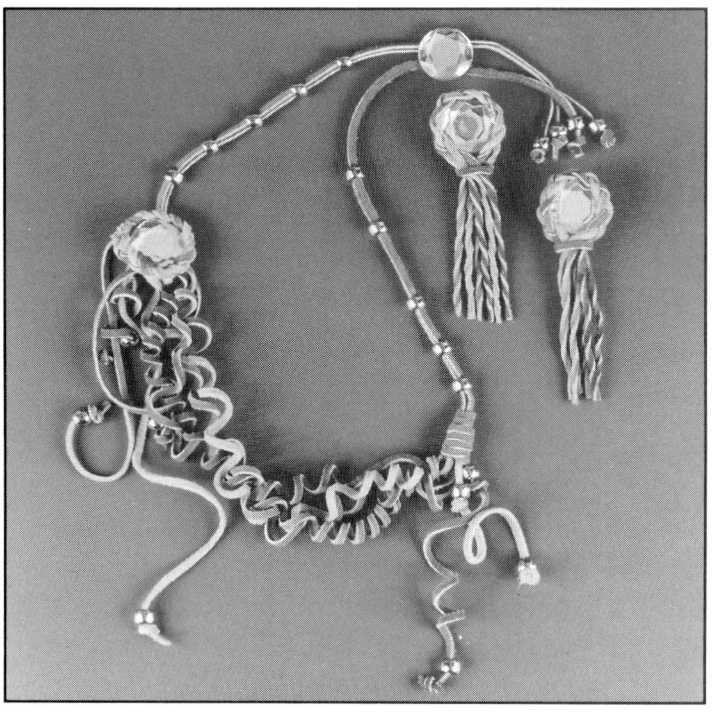

YOU WILL NEED:

suede lacing: $4\frac{2}{3}$ yards of mauve, $1\frac{1}{4}$ yards of peach, 2 yards of tan, 2 yards of pink
four 1" (28mm) clear round rhinestones
22 silver pony beads (necklace)
bolo tie slide (necklace)
2 earring posts
$\frac{3}{8}$" wide dowel or pencil
small bowl of water
paper towels
ruler
scissors
pliers
E-6000™ glue

1

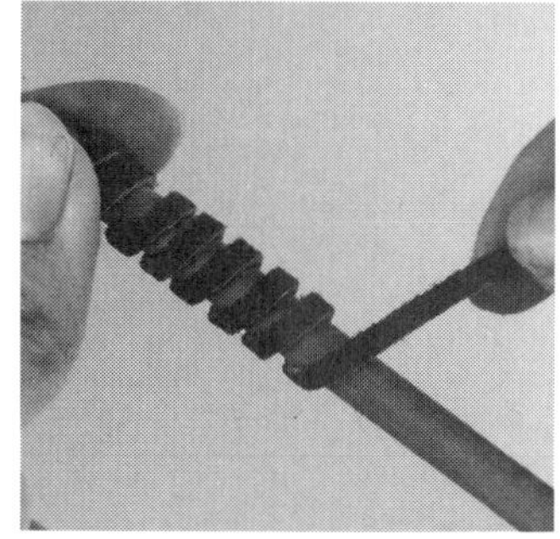

2

3

4

1 **For the necklace:** Cut a $3\frac{1}{2}$" length of each color lacing. Glue the lengths together at one end, braid, then glue the other ends together. Glue the braid around a rhinestone, bringing the ends to the back. Set aside for step 6.

2 Cut two 20" lengths of mauve lacing, one of tan, and one of peach. Soak in water, blot excess, and wrap tightly around the dowel. Let dry. These will be the center of the necklace. Cut two 7" mauve lengths, a 10" peach length, and an 8" tan length; curl as before and dry (group A). Cut a 7" peach length and a 10" mauve length; curl and dry (group B). Set aside for steps 5–7.

3 Cut two 14" lengths of mauve lacing and glue together to within $2\frac{1}{2}$" of one end. Slip a bead onto each unglued end and knot the end. Repeat with two 12" mauve lengths.

4 Glue the bolo slide to the back of a rhinestone. Insert the 14" glued length through the right side of the slide and the 12" glued length into the left side (use pliers to tighten the slide if needed). Slip five beads onto each side, spacing them 1" apart, beginning $1\frac{1}{2}$" below the rhinestone.

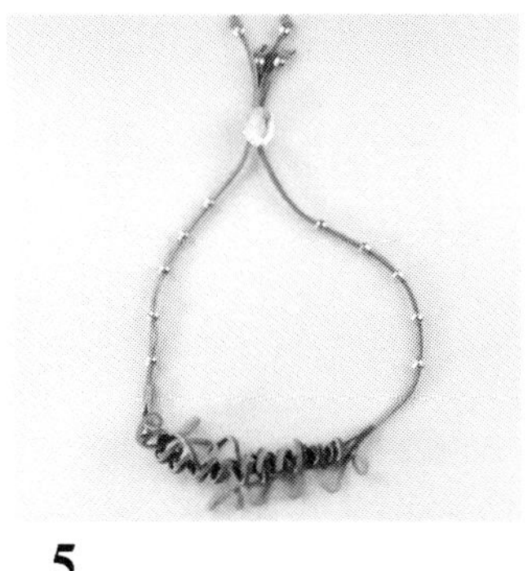

5

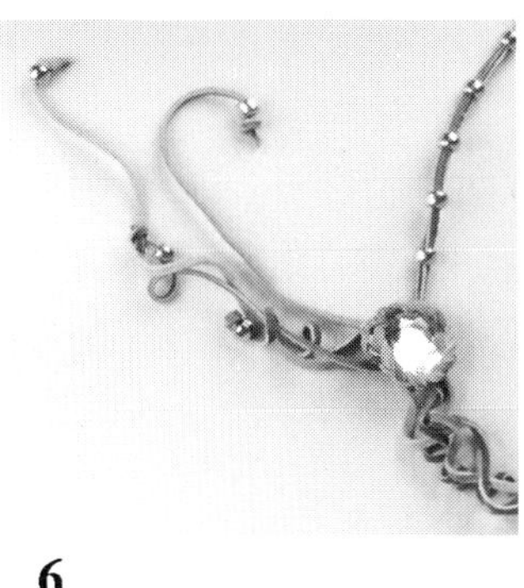

6

5 Glue the four 20" curled lengths from step 2 together at each end. Glue one end to the end of the 14" glued strand and the other to the end of the 12" glued strand.

6 Glue the group A curled lacing to the back of the braid-trimmed rhinestone from step 1. Slip a bead onto each length and knot the lacing end to secure it. Glue the rhinestone over the glued joint on the left side.

7

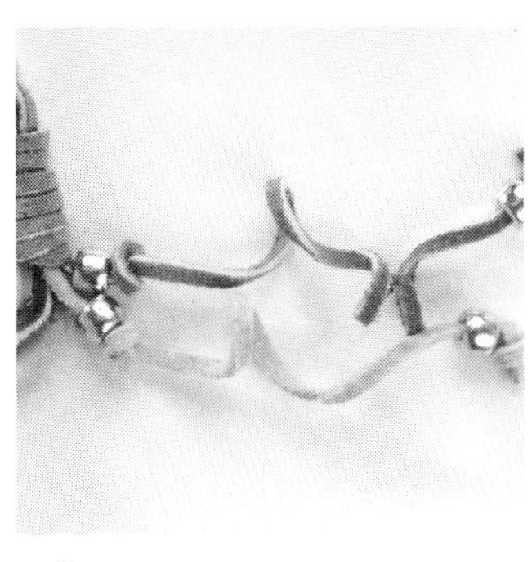

8

7 Glue the group B curled lacing to the right side joint. Cut an 8" length of mauve lacing and wrap it spiral-fashion around the joint, gluing each wrap.

8 Slip a bead onto each length, slide it up to the joint, and knot just below it. Slip another bead onto each length and knot the lacing end to secure it.

9

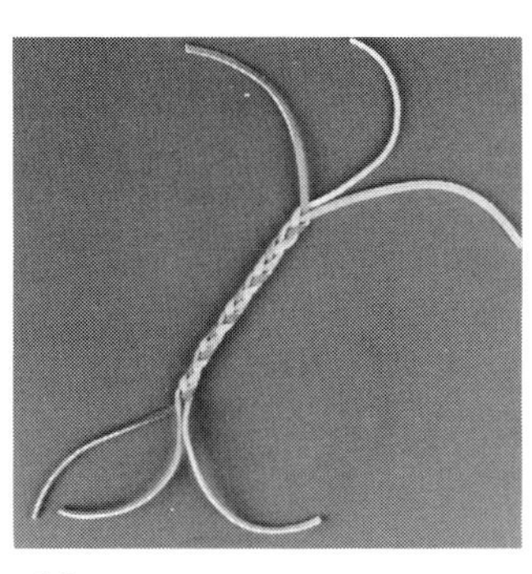

10

9 **For each earring:** Cut a 14" length of pink lacing. Coil, gluing to secure each coil. Glue a rhinestone onto the coil.

10 Cut an 18" length of each color lacing. Hold them together 4" from one end and braid for 4". Cut the tails to 4".

11 back view

12

11 Glue the braid around the rhinestone, gluing the braid ends (not the tails) together at the bottom. Cut a 1" length of mauve lacing and glue it around the top of the tails. Glue on an earring post.

12 Wet the tails, blot excess water, and twist each tail tightly. Hold until it will retain the twist when released.

COIL AND BANGLE BRACELETS

by Marie Le Fevre

YOU WILL NEED:

for the coil bracelet:
suede lacing: 60" of white, 40" of turquoise
9 silver pony beads
leather glue
for the bangle bracelet:
3½"x7" piece of pink leather
1"x6" metal bracelet blank
warm water, bowl, clothespins, paper towels
E-6000™ glue

1 **For the coil bracelet:** Cut four 10" lengths each of white and turquoise. Coil each around the dowel, gluing to secure each wrap. Let the glue dry, then remove the coils. Lay them on the table, alternating colors, with each coil overlapping the previous one by half. Weave the remaining white length in and out through the coils as shown in the diagram. Each time you bring the lacing to the top, add a silver bead.

2 Thread one end of the lacing through two beads, then knot the end. Thread the other lacing end through in the opposite direction and knot. Adjust the bracelet size by pulling in opposite directions.

3 **For the bangle bracelet:** Soak the leather in warm water for a few minutes, remove, and pat off excess water with paper towels. Place it wrong side up on a flat surface and center the bracelet blank on it. Apply glue along the center top of the blank and press one long edge of the leather into it.

4 Fold a ⅜" hem in the other long edge. Bring the hemmed edge over and glue it overlapping the previously glued edge. Crease and crinkle the leather, playing with it until you are pleased with the effect. Tuck in and glue the ends, holding them in place with clothespins. Bend the bracelet to fit your wrist; let dry.

1

2

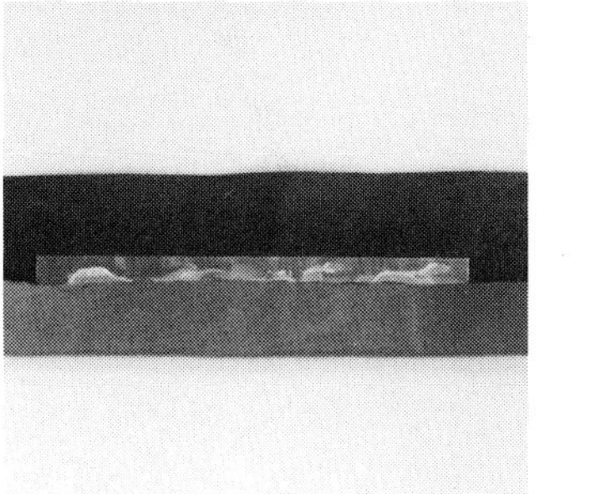

3

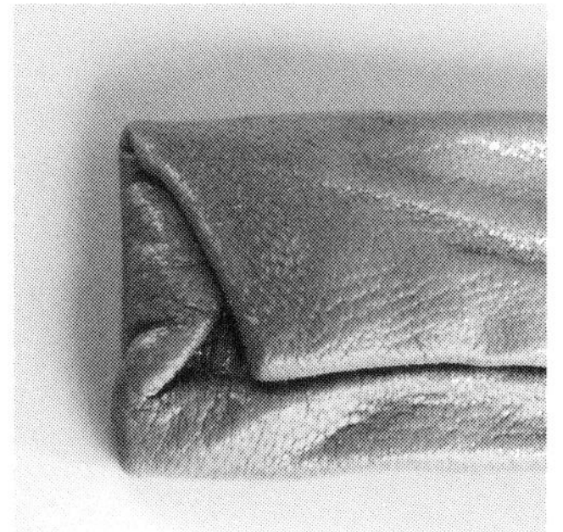

4

NAPKIN RINGS

by Marie Le Fevre

YOU WILL NEED:

ruler
scissors
leather glue
1½" wide x 1⅛" thick wooden napkin rings
for the concho napkin ring:
suede lacing: 1⅓ yards of peach, 1 yard of burgundy
one 1" wide round nickel concho —
for the beaded napkin ring:
suede lacing: 1¼ yards of beige, 24" of brown
9 silver pony beads

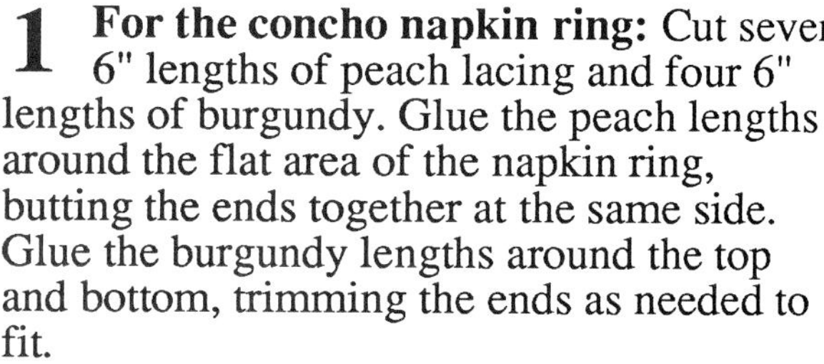

1 **For the concho napkin ring:** Cut seven 6" lengths of peach lacing and four 6" lengths of burgundy. Glue the peach lengths around the flat area of the napkin ring, butting the ends together at the same side. Glue the burgundy lengths around the top and bottom, trimming the ends as needed to fit.

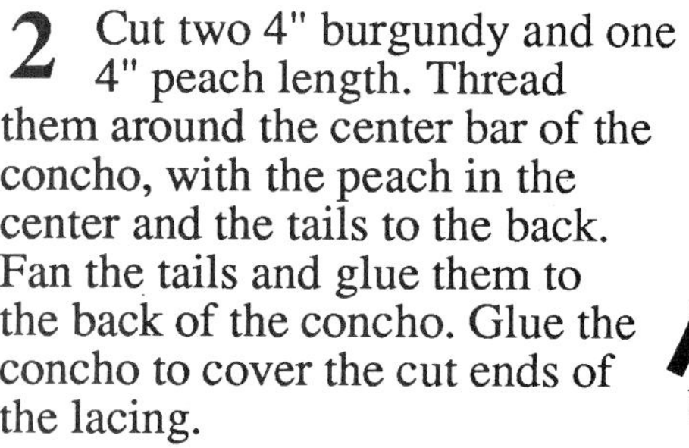

2 Cut two 4" burgundy and one 4" peach length. Thread them around the center bar of the concho, with the peach in the center and the tails to the back. Fan the tails and glue them to the back of the concho. Glue the concho to cover the cut ends of the lacing.

back view

1

2

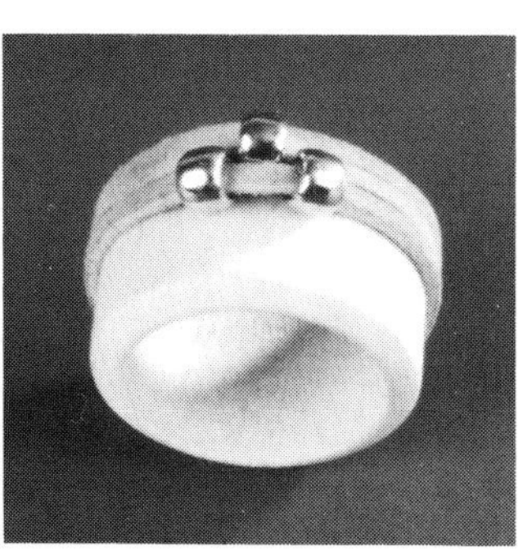

3

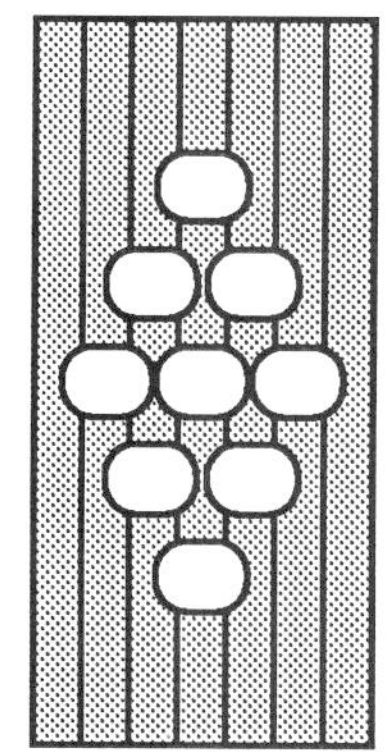

4

3 **For the beaded napkin ring:** Cut seven 6" lengths of beige lacing and four 6" lengths of brown. Glue a beige length along one edge of the flat area of the napkin ring. Slide a bead to the center of another beige length, then glue it next to the first—do not glue for ¼" on each side of the bead. Slide two beads to the center of the third beige length, positioning them ½" apart. Glue next to the last length.

4 Follow the diagram to continue gluing beaded lengths; finish with a plain length. Glue the brown lengths around the top and bottom, trimming the ends as needed.

COASTERS

by Marie Le Fevre

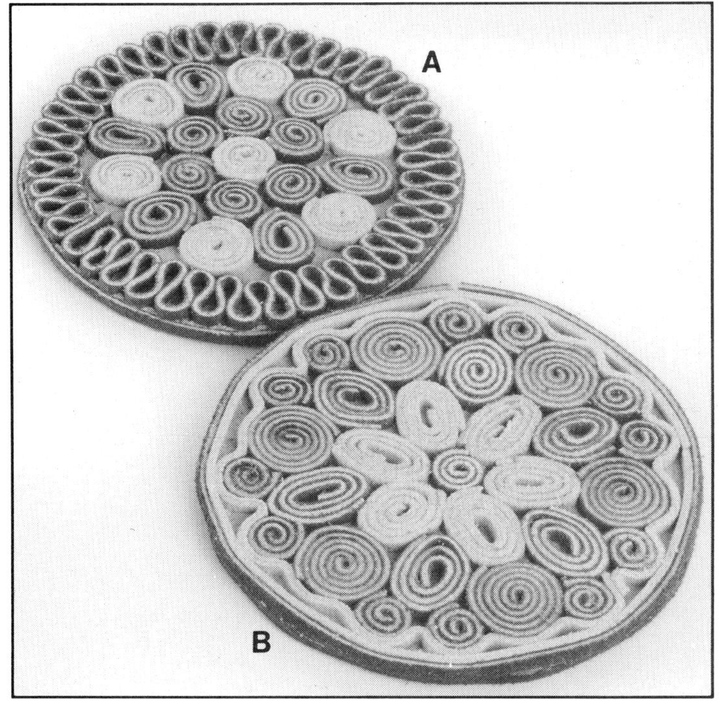

YOU WILL NEED:

two 4" leather circles (pattern inside the back cover)
¼" wide dowel or pencil
suede lacing for coaster A: 2½ yards of burgundy, 1 yard of peach, 24" of brown, 18" of dark brown
suede lacing for coaster B: 1 yard of burgundy, 2 yards of peach, 1½ yards of brown, 2 yards of dark brown
pencil
ruler
scissors
leather glue

COLOR KEY: peach burgundy brown dk. brown

1

2

1 **Coaster A:** Mark the center of the circle. Measure and mark a border ½" from the outer edge. Glue burgundy lacing in a zig-zag pattern around the border; cut off excess. Follow the diagram to lay out the coils—do not glue until the design is complete. Coil a 4" peach length (center). Coil six 3" lengths of dark brown (first row). Coil six 5" peach lengths; loosely coil six 4" brown lengths and pinch them into ovals (outer row). Glue in place. Glue the remaining burgundy leather around the edge of the leather circle.

2 **Coaster B:** Mark the center of the circle. Follow the diagram to lay out the coils on the leather circle—do not glue until the design is complete. Coil a 2" length of burgundy (center). Loosely coil six 5" lengths of peach (first row). Loosely coil six 5" lengths of burgundy (second row) and pinch these into ovals. Coil six 7" brown lengths and twelve 2" dark brown lengths (outer row). Glue, taking care to leave a ⅛" border around the outside edge of the leather circle. Cut an 18" peach length and glue around the coils, bending the lacing to conform to the shapes. Trim excess. Cut a 13" peach length and glue it around the 18" length in a smooth circle. Cut two 13" dark brown lengths and glue them around the outer edge, one on top of the other.

ROUND CORD NECKLACE/HEART PIN

by E. Wayne Fox

YOU WILL NEED:

ruler
scissors
for the necklace:
round leather lacing cord: 2 yards of red, 2 yards of black
18 silver heart pony beads
3/8" wide half-round nickel press-on stud
for the pin:
8" length of black suede lacing
1 1/4" wide nickel heart concho with horizontal slots
heart pony beads: 4 silver, 2 black
1" long pin back
E-6000™ glue

1

2

3

4

1 **For the necklace:** Begin with the red cord. Make a knot 6" from one end. Insert the other end through two beads and slide them up to the knot. Knot again on the other side of the beads, as shown. Measure down 3 1/2", knot, add two beads, and knot; repeat for a total of five bead/knot sets. Cut the cord 6" past the last knot. Repeat with the black cord, but begin 8" from the end and make only four bead/knot sets; cut the cord 8" past the last knot.

2 Place the stud face down. Overlap the red cord ends 1/2" over the stud. Repeat with the black cord ends, then press the prongs down to clamp the ends securely.

3 **For the pin:** Glue the pin to the back of the concho bar. Fold the lacing in half and pass the fold through the top slot from front to back, then back through the bottom slot. Push both ends of the lacing through the loop and pull to tighten it around the bar and pin (lark's head knot).

4 Slide a silver, a black, and another silver bead onto one lacing end. Knot the lacing to secure the beads. Repeat with the other end.

SEVEN-HEART NECKLACE

by E. Wayne Fox

YOU WILL NEED:

3 yards of violet suede lacing
nickel heart conchos with horizontal slots:
four 1¼" wide, three 1" wide
20 silver pony beads
E-6000™ glue

1

2

4

1 Cut a 27" lacing length for the necklace. For the fringe, cut two 11", four 10", and two 7" lengths. Fold each fringe length in half and slip a silver bead over both ends, sliding it up until a ¼" loop projects.

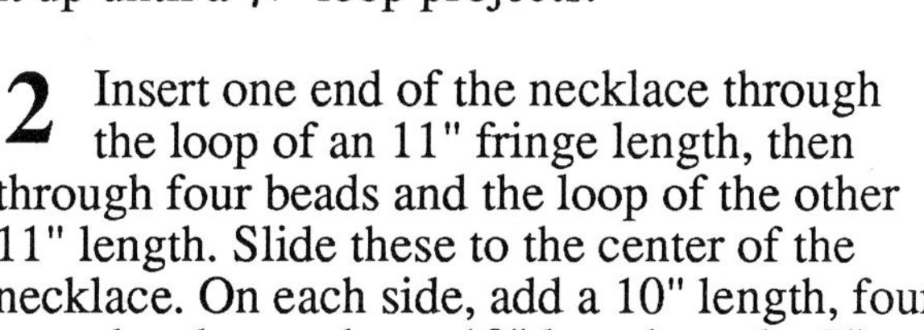

2 Insert one end of the necklace through the loop of an 11" fringe length, then through four beads and the loop of the other 11" length. Slide these to the center of the necklace. On each side, add a 10" length, four more beads, another a 10" length, and a 7" length.

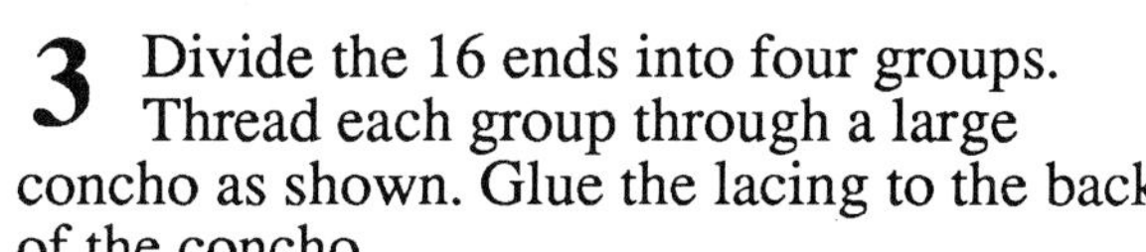

3 Divide the 16 ends into four groups. Thread each group through a large concho as shown. Glue the lacing to the back of the concho.

4 Take the four center lacing ends (the 11" lengths) and thread them through a small concho, gluing to secure. Repeat with the next four to the right (10" lengths), then with the next four to the left.

3

BUTTON COVERS & CONCHO EARRINGS

by Marie Le Fevre

YOU WILL NEED:

ruler
scissors
for the button covers:
suede lacing: 3 1/2 yards of tan, 1 1/3 yards of gray, 1 1/3 yards of tan
four 6mm turquoise rhinestones
four 5/8" wide button covers
leather glue
E-6000™ glue
for the concho earrings:
6" of black suede lacing
one 2 1/2"x2 3/4" oval turquoise suede concho
one 1 3/4"x2 1/8" oval brass concho
gold beads: twenty-two 2mm, two 3mm, four 6mm
two black pony beads
two clip earring backs
tin snips
E-6000™ glue

1

2

1 **For each button cover:** Cut an 8" length of tan. Coil it, gluing to secure each wrap. Glue the coil to the top of a button cover, then glue a rhinestone in the center.

2 Cut a 16" length of each color. Hold together, tape one end, and braid. Glue one end of the braid to the button cover. Wrap and glue it around, cutting off the excess. Use extra glue to secure the ends.

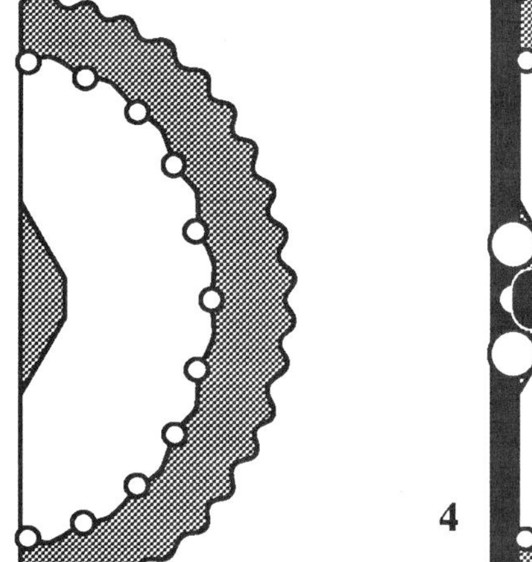

3

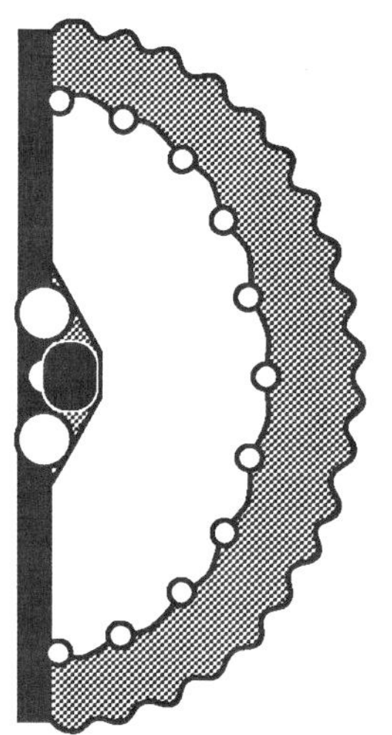

4

3 **For the earrings:** Use tin snips to cut the brass concho in half and to cut off the bar. Cut the suede concho in half. Glue the brass halves onto the suede halves, with the cut edges even. Glue a 2mm bead to the inner point of each brass scallop.

4 Cut the black lacing into two 3" lengths and glue one along the cut edge of a suede concho. Glue a pony bead to the inner curve, with the hole toward the black lacing. Glue a 3mm bead into the hole, then glue a 6mm bead above and below. Glue a clip to the upper back. Repeat for the other earring.

DOVE ORNAMENT

by Marie Le Fevre

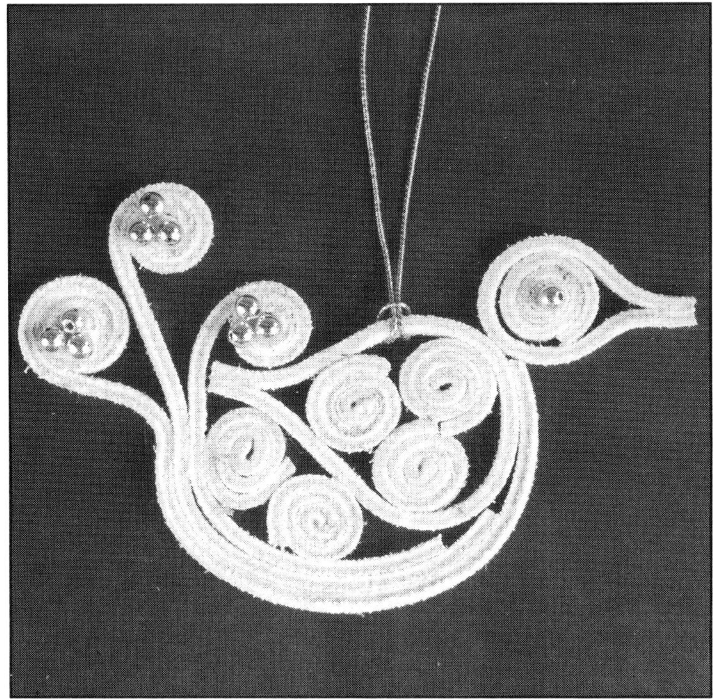

YOU WILL NEED:

42" length of white suede lacing
8" length of gold thread
ten 3mm gold beads
leather glue
E-6000™ glue
ruler
scissors

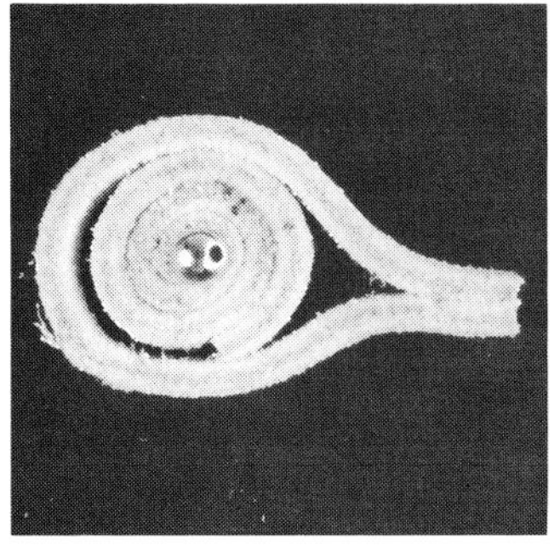

1

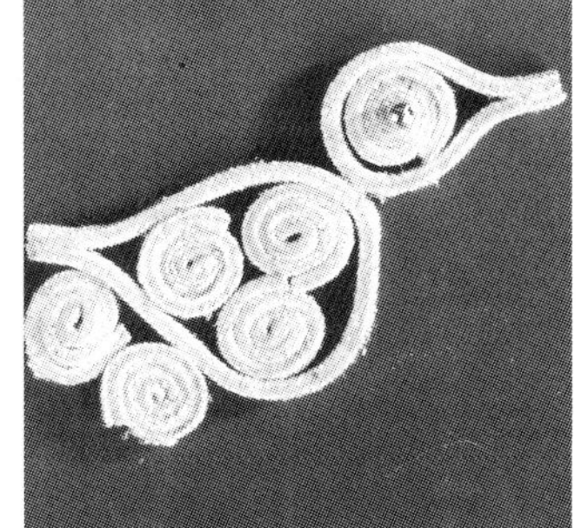

2

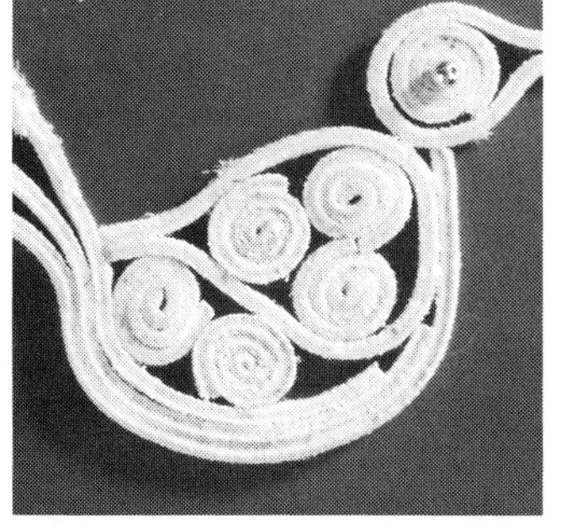

3

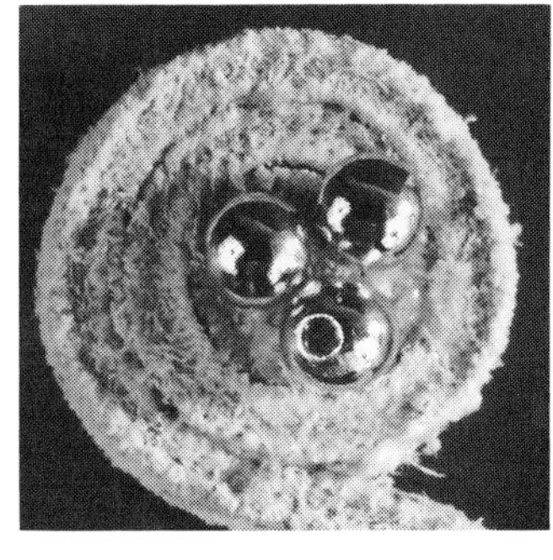

4

1 Cut six 2½" lacing lengths. Coil each, gluing to secure each coil. **For the head:** Cut a 3" length. Glue it around one coil, gluing the ends together into a beak. Glue a bead to the coil center for the eye.

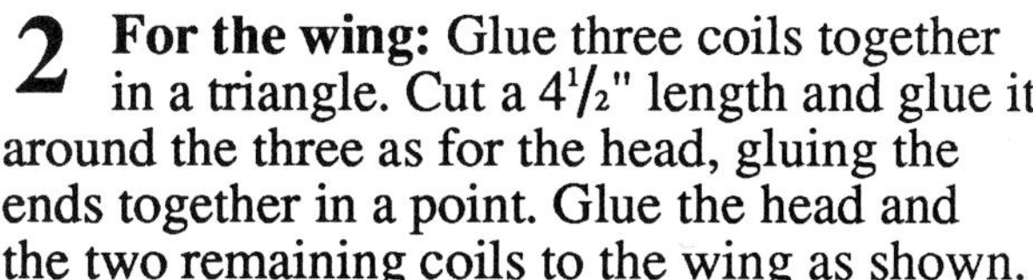

2 **For the wing:** Glue three coils together in a triangle. Cut a 4½" length and glue it around the three as for the head, gluing the ends together in a point. Glue the head and the two remaining coils to the wing as shown.

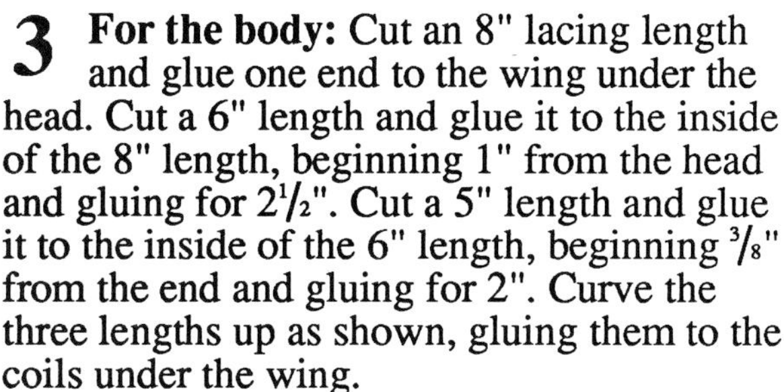

3 **For the body:** Cut an 8" lacing length and glue one end to the wing under the head. Cut a 6" length and glue it to the inside of the 8" length, beginning 1" from the head and gluing for 2½". Cut a 5" length and glue it to the inside of the 6" length, beginning ⅜" from the end and gluing for 2". Curve the three lengths up as shown, gluing them to the coils under the wing.

4 Coil the end of each length and glue as shown. Glue three beads in a triangle to the center of each coil. **For a hanger:** Knot the ends of the gold cord together, then attach it to the dove's back in a lark's head knot, as shown in the large photo.

ANGEL ORNAMENT

by Marie Le Fevre

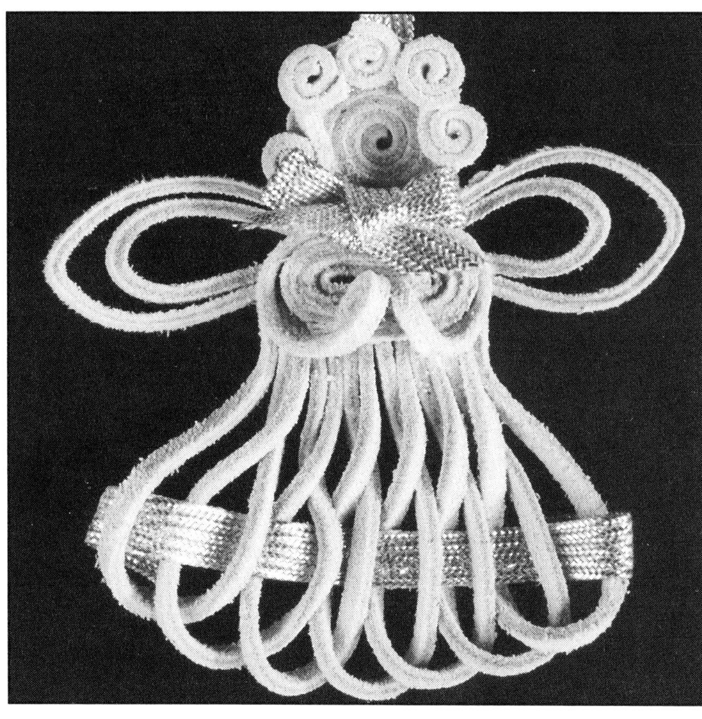

YOU WILL NEED:

$2^1/_3$ yards of white suede lacing
$^1/_2$ yard of $^3/_8$" wide flat silver braid
leather glue

1 **For the skirt:** Cut seven 7" lacing lengths. Form each into a loop and glue the ends together. Glue the tops together as shown. **For the wings:** Cut a 14" length. Fold it back and forth to make two inner $1^1/_2$" loops and two 2" outer loops. Glue together at the center, then glue it to the top of the skirt. **For the head:** Cut an 8" length and coil it, gluing each coil. Glue it to the center top of the wings.

2 **For the body:** Cut an 8" length. Fold one end in $^1/_2$"; coil the rest around the folded end, forming an oval. Glue it over the area where the wings and skirt join. **For the hands:** Cut a 4" length and coil each end to make a $^1/_4$" wide "hand." Glue the center to the top of the body. Bring the hands together as if praying; glue to secure.

3 **For the hair:** Cut a 4" length; coil each end as for the hands. Glue it to the head front, with a coil extending down each side (black area of diagram). Cut three 3" lengths. Coil and glue them, then glue them across the center top for bangs (gray areas).

4 Cut a 6" length of braid and use it to tie a shoestring bow with $^1/_2$" loops. Trim the tails diagonally to $^1/_2$" long and glue it to her neck. Cut a 5" braid length. Arrange the skirt loops to overlap, then weave the braid in and out through them as shown in the large photo. Fold the braid ends to the skirt back and glue. Fold the remaining braid in half and glue the ends to the back for a hanger.

1

2

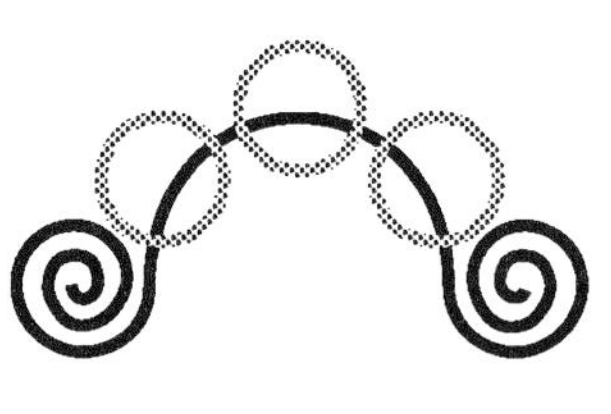

3

4 back view

COIL ORNAMENTS

by Marie Le Fevre

YOU WILL NEED:

leather glue
E-6000™
for the tree:
suede lacing: 40" of green, 10" of red
1 gold pony bead
eighteen 3mm gold beads
10" length of gold cord (hanger)
for the wreath:
suede lacing: 64" of green, 20" of red
twelve 3mm gold beads
1/8" wide dowel or thin pencil
8" length of gold cord (hanger)

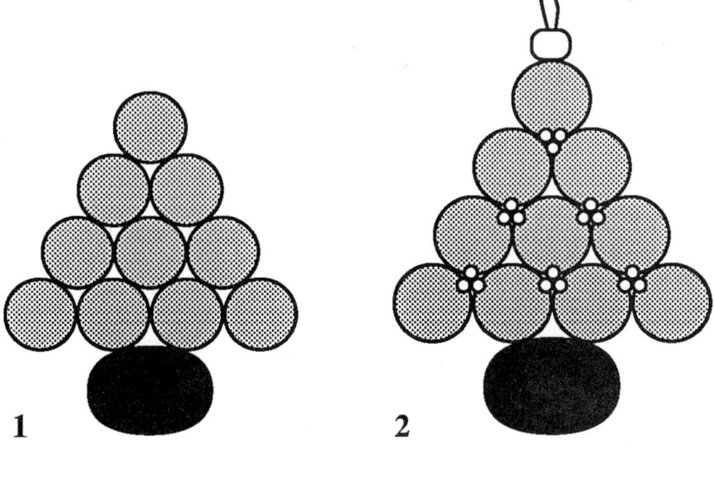

3

4

(a)

(b)

1 **For the tree:** Cut the green lacing into ten 4" lengths. Coil each length, gluing to secure each wrap. Fold one end of the red lacing in 3/8" and glue to secure. Coil the rest around the glued section, gluing each wrap, to form an oval coil. Assemble as shown in the diagram, gluing at the contact points.

2 Glue the pony bead to the tree top with the hole going up and down. Knot the hanger ends together and glue the knot into the hole. Glue groups of three 3mm beads as shown.

3 **For the wreath:** Cut the green lacing into sixteen 4" lengths. Coil and glue as in step 1. Place nine in a circle; glue at the contact points. Glue the remaining seven coils and groups of three beads as shown.

4 For the bow: (a) Cut two 5 1/2" red lengths. Coil each around the dowel, gluing to secure each wrap. Remove the dowel and pinch the coils into teardrops; glue together at the points. (b) Cut an 8" red length. Fold and glue as shown. Cut a 1" red length and wrap it around the bow center as shown in the photo. Glue the point of the 8" length to the back. Glue the bow to the wreath. Knot the hanger ends together, then tie it around the wreath and bow as shown.

SIX-STRAND NECKLACE

by E. Wayne Fox

YOU WILL NEED:

$5\frac{1}{3}$ yards of burgundy suede lacing
one $1\frac{3}{4}$"x$2\frac{1}{8}$" oval brass concho
pony beads: 36 black, 12 gold
10 pink heart pony beads
ruler
scissors
leather glue

1

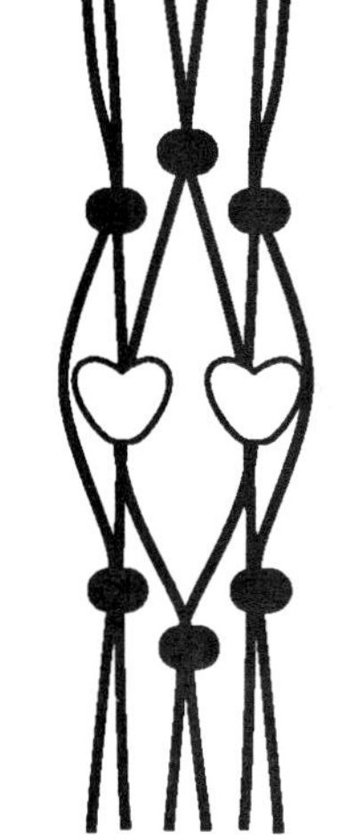

2

3

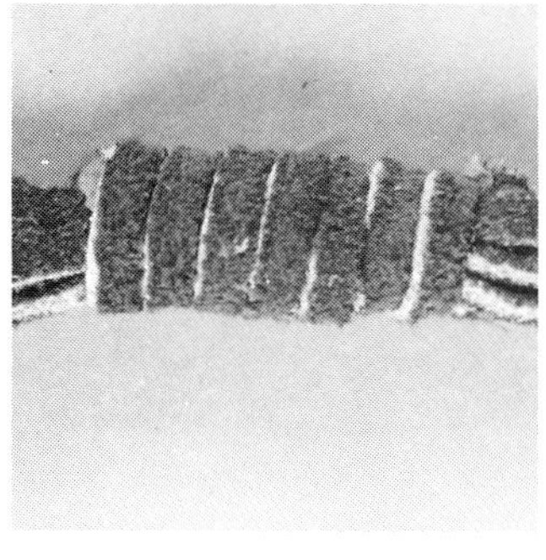

4

1 Cut the lacing into one 12" and six 30" strands; set the 12" strand aside for step 4. Knot one 30" strand at the center, then handle all the 30" strands as one to thread one end through the concho as shown. Position the concho 8" from the end.

2 Follow the diagram to thread the short lacing ends through six black beads and two heart beads. The center bottom black bead will be 1" above the concho.

3 Select one of the unknotted long ends and add beads in this order: one gold, two black, one heart, two black, and one gold. Be sure the top of the heart points toward the concho. Slide the beads up to the concho, then knot the strand below the last bead. Repeat on two more strands, knotting the second 4" below the concho and the third even with the center knot made in step 1.

4 Follow the same order to thread beads onto the strand knotted in step 1, but have the top of the heart point toward the end of the strand. Knot one of the remaining unknotted strands 8" from the end, the other 12" from the end. Follow the same order to string beads onto these strands. Follow the step 2 diagram to thread the lacing ends through six black and two heart beads. The center top bead will be 3" below the strand ends. Overlap the right and left strand ends $\frac{1}{2}$" and glue them together. Wrap and glue the 12" strand around the ends.